Waiting *for* God *to* Fill *the* Cradle

A Four Week Devotional for Couples

by Eric and April Motl

Waiting for God to Fill the Cradle: Devotionals for Couples
Published by Motl Ministry Publications Copyright © 2008 by April Motl revised 2011

To order additional copies, write Motl Ministries - email: info@motlministries.com

Table of Contents

_____

Preface
4

Introduction
5

Preface

In this book you will find that over the course of the next four weeks there is a theme and a key point for you to ponder as an individual and as a couple for that particular week. Some of these points might be more important for your spouse than you, but as you read, be open to how the Lord might be giving you a deeper understanding of your spouse's emotional/spiritual needs during this season of waiting. Be open to what the Lord wants to accomplish through this time in you as an individual and as a couple. God doesn't waste anything - including this struggle.

Each week includes five days of devotional reading, one day of couples questions and one day of Scripture prayers. The idea behind this is that two days out of the week you and your beloved will come together with open honest hearts for discussion and prayer. If you can, pray together everyday. It is a blessing and a safeguard for your marriage.

We are praying for God's love and goodness to surround you, His will to be revealed in your hearts and for His truth to free you.

The themes and points to ponder for each week:

Week One
Theme: God is the Giver of Children
Points to Ponder: Knowing that bearing children has nothing to do with me and everything to do with God's

perfect plan frees me up from guilt and self-focused thinking. It also fixes my eyes on the Lord.

Week Two
Theme: Finding my Identity and Direction in God's Word

Points to Ponder: Infertility has profound emotional impact on the way we see ourselves and our life purpose. Rooting our perspective in God's Word is our ultimate source of hope and healing.

Week Three
Theme: Where to put the Disappointment

Points to Ponder: Scripture records the struggle of many people who wanted children. From them we can learn how to maintain a healthy perspective on
this painful topic.

Week Four
Theme: Mining for the Gold During this Season of Waiting

Points to Ponder: If we are faithful to seek God during this time of waiting we will mine lasting gold for our lives so that this time will count for something!

Introduction

"Do you have children?"

It seems as though the frequency of the question should numb the sting - but it doesn't. Whether your wait for a baby feels like an eternity or has just begun, the issue of infertility, or struggling to conceive, reaches far and wide across our own identities, our relationships with friends and family, our marriage and even our relationship with God.

Your Identity

Facing down infertility can deeply impact your identity. Thoughts like, *is God withholding blessing from me?* or *Maybe I would just make a really bad parent,* can fill our day-to-day thoughts. I've also had my share of "I must be crazy" thoughts as I tracked and clocked every little symptom, sure with each one that this was the month I was pregnant - only to find that it was, yet again, a false alarm.

Beside all the thoughts that fill our minds, there can be heavy guilt associated with not being pregnant. My heart has ached as I have wrongly absorbed responsibility for not getting pregnant. I remember two women who jeeringly asked, "What's the matter with you? Why can't you give your husband children?" I had a relative I love very much ask me if "it hurt enough yet?" She went on to ridicule me because I hadn't gotten pregnant yet and said that if it hurt enough maybe I would finally go do "what was right" and get the needed procedures done. She was misinformed about the circumstances surrounding our empty cradle and her words cut deeply.

For some couples, past failures or hurts rear their ugly head. Abortions and STDs can increase the difficulty in having children, further compounding a sense of guilt. Sexual baggage from personal choices or abuse can get tossed into the issue of processing infertility. The empty cradle has a profoundly deep emotional impact. In order to maintain a Biblical view of yourself in the midst of this circumstance, here are a few stabilizing practices:

1. *Confess wrong thinking about issues of guilt as they come up (1 John 1:9)*. If past mistakes have had a long-term affect on your fertility (we are not saying this is the case, but it is best to cover all the bases when considering what God might be doing in you life), ask God to forgive you and then live in His grace! This won't necessarily solve your medical concerns, but it will bring *spiritual* healing and peace. And remember, no one is perfect. We're all sinners in need of grace. Confessing our past mistakes to God is a healthy practice *all* Christians should maintain across various life-circumstances, not just infertility issues. By the way, it is possible that even thinking our infertility is our fault can be wrongful thinking (i.e., sin). If you have wrongly taken responsibility for your infertility, ask God to purify your thinking with His truth for this too.

2. *Talk and pray with your spouse, a mentor, ministry leader, Christian counselor,* or all of the above, in order to Scripturally process any old baggage your empty cradle might be stirring up *(Proverbs 15:22)*.

3. *Root your identity in what the Bible says about you (John 17:17)*.

Your Marriage

When a couple sets out to start a family it is devastating to come up month after month with a negative sign on the pregnancy test. But in the middle of the disappointment

7

there can be good things that come your way. While you and your spouse are waiting, try these ideas:

1. Pray about three qualities you want your future family to have and then spend time developing them. Example: my husband and I wanted to grow in our finances so we went through a Christian video seminar together about financial freedom.

2. Celebrate this time together! Do things you wouldn't normally do with kids -- take a non-kid-friendly vacation, make love somewhere you wouldn't if you had kids in the house, encourage each other to pursue goals that you might not pursue if you had kids right now.

3. Communicate! Talk to each other about your feelings (but be sensitive about the timing you pick for your conversations). Because this is such a deeply emotional topic give your spouse time to process before you jump into a conversation.

4. Pray together! Talk to the Lord together about what you are feeling and commit your desires to Him. If your situation warrants it, prayerfully consider options like adoption or foster care.

Your Relationship with God

Your empty cradle affects your life in many ways. But how you let it affect your perception of God will ripple through every other facet of your life. If we wrongly take responsibility for our infertility, it is because we do not understand that *God* is the Giver of life. If we blame our spouse or allow the disappointment to pull our marriage apart, we put our husband/wife on the throne of our hearts instead of giving God His rightful place within us. Your relationship with the Lord will be the solid rock, enabling you to weather the storm of dis-appointment that comes from not having children (or not having them on your timescale). Here are some ideas to help you seek His face in this circumstance:

1. Be honest with God; He has big enough shoulders for you to give Him your hurts.

2. Study the places in the Bible where a couple didn't have children. Ask yourself, *what was God developing in this couple, what did He want them to learn about Him and themselves through infertility.* Studying this has been such a blessing of hope to us!

3. Pray for a baby! Scripture details many couples who wanted children and prayed for one. We have dear friends who conceived after years of an empty womb when they asked for others to pray for them.

4. Learn contentedness. Life is full of waiting and you will be a much better parent and individual if you learn the secret of contentedness in the circumstances God brings your way. We find in Scripture that often times God gives us the desires of our hearts when we are most content with Him and Him alone.

5. Be open to the Potter's hand. Seek to give and bend to God's shaping hand in your life. Embrace what He is doing and ask Him for the grace to live, feel, and think about these circumstances in accordance with His plan for your life.

6. Trust God! The Lord is up to something good in your life (Romans 8:28)! My husband and I have talked about some of the purposes God might have for not giving us children. We may or may not be right, but we understand that our lack of children does not equate to an absence of God's purpose or work in our lives.

Amidst the charting of temperatures and (other unmentionables) may you find that place of peace in God; may your marriage grow in this season and may you be richly blessed as you wait on God to fill your cradle.

Week One

Theme: God is the Giver of Children
Points to Ponder: Knowing that bearing children has nothing to do with me and everything to do with God's perfect plan frees me up from guilt and self-focused thinking. It also fixes my eyes on the Lord rather than my circumstances.

●————————————●

Day One
God is the Giver of Life

Now the man had relations with his wife Eve, and she conceived and gave birth to Cain, and she said, "I have gotten a manchild with the help of the LORD." Genesis 4:1

From the very first birth, it is recorded that the miracle of life is indeed a gift from God. It is by His hand that life is created and only by God's help that children are born. As a young person, I was taught that becoming pregnant is incredibly easy and the hard part is *not* getting pregnant. Maybe you also expected that pregnancy would be as "easy as fallin' off a log", and now feel the angst of those expectations colliding with reality.

Research shows that a woman's egg is available for fertilization for only about 12 to 24 hours. Since sperm can live 3-5 days, that widens the fertility window to about 5-7 days.[1] Those odds, compounded with a myriad of physical

11

circumstances which could hamper conception, also considering the pregnancy process and the statistics on miscarriage, make the birth of a baby nothing short of a true miracle.

As you walk this journey of waiting for a baby, focus on the One who gives life instead of focusing on all the things you need to do in order to get pregnant. This Biblical ground is more solid to stand on than what the world says or promises. Invite God into the process. Pray while you go about your "baby making" and fix your eyes on Jesus every step of the way; because it is only "with the help of the Lord" that anyone can ever have a child.

[1] www.Americanpregnancy.org

Day Two
God Works in Impossible Situations

So Boaz took Ruth, and she became his wife, and he went in to her. And the LORD enabled her to conceive, and she gave birth to a son. Ruth 4:12-13

Ruth was a widow who left her homeland to journey with her mother-in-law, Naomi, back to Israel. She had no hope for a husband, a family, or happiness outside of her relationship with the Lord and Naomi. She committed her life to the Lord and most likely expected that as a widowed foreigner she would have a hard and lonely future ahead. However, the Lord was not done with these two women! As Ruth worked the dusty fields, picking up the bits of grain left behind by the harvesters, the Lord turned a certain man's gaze in her direction. Within a few short weeks this young widowed woman was married to a kind, godly man. While Scripture does not describe the length of time it took before they had a little one on the way, we are told that it was the Lord's doing.

Both Ruth and Naomi were coming from places of profound emptiness and grief. They had both lost husbands; Naomi lost her only two sons and Ruth was childless. Losing a spouse or a child is always a grievous experience, but during this time period in history it also meant that these women were utterly destitute. Naomi, whose name means *sweet*, renamed herself Mara or *bitter* because she felt so empty (Ruth 1:21).

The process of trying to have a baby in the face of months piling upon months, years upon years, without that longed

Journaling your Journey ~

_____

_____

_____

_____

_____

_____

_____

_____

_____

_____

_____

_____

_____

_____

_____

_____

_____

_____

_____

_____

_____

_____

for result can leave us feeling profoundly empty as well. As my husband and I go through this process together, I often feel the ache of emptiness and my total powerlessness over the situation.

If you feel like there is a big sign over your life that says "NEVER- you are in good company!

However, Ruth's story has great encouragement in it for those of us who wish for our empty cradles to be filled. We can relate to her total dependency on God. We can identify with her sense of emptiness. Ruth was a foreign woman who expected to never have a husband, never have a family... all these never, never, nevers! If you feel like there is a big sign over your life that says "NEVER"- you are in good company! God tends to step in most when we realize we can't take another step without Him. He specializes in those impossible situations! Naomi and Ruth had no idea what God was up to. They could not see that just around the bend in the road God would send someone to take care of their needs and fill their desires. God is up to something good in your life right now even if you can't see it! If your knees are bent and your face brought low, take heart. He sees you and is working on your behalf! May He fill that which is empty with His presence and hope today!

Journaling your Journey ~

_____

_____

_____

_____

_____

_____

_____

_____

_____

_____

_____

_____

_____

_____

_____

_____

_____

_____

_____

_____

_____

Day Three
God Gives Children in His Time

Then the LORD took note of Sarah as He had said, and the LORD did for Sarah as He had promised. So Sarah conceived and bore a son to Abraham in his old age, at the appointed time of which God had spoken to him. Genesis 21:1-2

While there are days when I feel as though waiting for a baby has been an eternity, the life of Sarah and Abraham should bring all of us "waiters" a pick-me-up of hope. Abraham and Sarah waited 25 years for the Lord to fulfill His promise of a child. Both Abraham and Sarah were past childbearing years; certainly Sarah at 90 is not your typical age for becoming a mom! But God had a plan that He executed in His timing.

Before the time was right, Abraham and Sarah were on a long journey of faith. They had lessons to learn and mistakes to make. While Scripture does not expressly denote God's reason for taking so long to fulfill His promise, we can be sure it was for their good. Perhaps God was growing Abraham and Sarah into the kind of parents Isaac, their son, would need. After all, Isaac would be the first child in a special, promised heritage (see Genesis 12). No doubt their place as parents would be a very important role.

> *God gives children in His time. Be open to His plan and timing for your life.*

God gives children in His time. Be open to His plan and timing for your life. Ask Him to show you areas you need to grow in as an individual and in your marriage. Submit your schedule to His. He has you and your possible future children's best interest at heart. Who knows how special your possible future child may be (like Isaac)! And how important it is for their future success that you, as parents, be equipped and ready to raise them up in the Lord.

Journaling your Journey ~

_____

_____

_____

_____

_____

_____

_____

_____

_____

_____

_____

_____

_____

_____

_____

_____

_____

_____

_____

Day Four
God Gives Children for His Purposes

Now the LORD saw that Leah was unloved, and He opened her womb, but Rachel was barren. Leah conceived and bore a son and named him Reuben, for she said, "Because the LORD has seen my affliction; surely now my husband will love me." Then she conceived again and bore a son and said, "Because the LORD has heard that I am unloved, He has therefore given me this son also." So she named him Simeon. She conceived again and bore a son and said, "Now this time my husband will become attached to me, because I have borne him three sons." Therefore he was named Levi. And she conceived again and bore a son and said, "This time I will praise the LORD." Therefore she named him Judah. Then she stopped bearing. Genesis 29:31-35

During a time in Israel's history when it was not expressly stated that marriage should be between just two people, many men took more than one wife. In this case, it was two sisters (can you even imagine the squabbles?!). Rachel was the one that Jacob loved. But he had been deceived into marrying her older sister, Leah, as well. God saw Leah's plight and gave her children. Yet, with each birth Leah was trying to get something from her husband rather than from God. She thought each baby might bring her the love, affection, and approval her heart craved from Jacob.

When we first started trying to have children there were a number of things I (April) wanted to "get" from having children. One of those things was purpose in life. The Lord stopped me in my tracks and made me see my wrong thinking. A helpless baby cannot help me find my purpose! If God were to entrust me with a child, it would be my responsibility to help that little one find his or her purpose *in Christ*. The only way I will be able to do this successfully is to have already found *my purpose* in Christ too. Anything other than this line of thinking could have led me to idolize having children instead of finding my sole purpose in the Lord.

By the time Leah had four children she finally relented in trying to make her children meet her needs. With the fourth baby she declared that now, no strings attached, she would simply praise the Lord.

We have watched many people try to use their children in someway or another to meet their needs. God does not give children to meet our needs. God gives children to parents to serve the needs of their children so that they will grow up to be followers and servants of Jesus Christ. Is there something you want to "get" from having children? This is a tough one, but be honest with yourself. God wants to be your complete satisfaction. In your best interest, He might withhold something from you so that you will learn this. This is not necessarily the reason behind any of our empty cradles, but we found it important in our own lives to make sure that we had pure motives behind our wanting a family. Spend some time in prayer asking God to reveal and remove from your heart any wrong expectations or motives you might have about having children.

> *This line of thinking could have led me to idolize having children instead of finding my sole purpose in the Lord*

Journaling your Journey ~

_____

_____

_____

_____

_____

_____

_____

_____

_____

_____

_____

_____

_____

_____

_____

_____

_____

_____

_____

Day Five
God Gives Children in His Own Way

"Shout for joy, O barren one, you who have borne no child; break forth into joyful shouting...for the sons of the desolate one will be more numerous than the sons of the married woman," says the LORD. Isaiah 54:1

It was Sunday and right after church I (April) was going to a baby shower. I was thrilled and happy for my dear friend, but dreading the questions, comments and possible criticism from the other ladies at the shower concerning our not yet having children. So that morning as I got ready for church and the festivities to follow, I was mentally rehearsing gracious answers for that dreaded question about when I was going to "get with it" and have babies. That same morning right after the worship in our youth service a couple of our girls took the stage. One of them curled her finger at me, motioning for me to join them. Not sure what to expect, I came. It was minister appreciation month and the students from our youth ministry wanted to honor my husband and I for our service. I was so surprised (they hadn't done that before) I had to blink back the tears.

> *God wants to be your complete satisfaction. In your best interest, He might withhold something from you so that you will learn this lesson.*

I didn't have children in the normal sense of the word, but I had the privilege of pouring my heart into these students. We didn't yet have a family to leave a legacy of faith with, but we had younger brothers and sisters in Christ to serve and encourage in their faith. If God chooses to give us children, I will rejoice! But for today, Eric and I praise God for the opportunities He has graciously given us to serve His kids. I thanked Him for that perfectly timed reminder right before the baby shower - that God can give us "children" in a variety of ways!

How else could God make the childless woman to have more "sons" than the woman filled with a family? I have known other women who could not have children who also worked extensively with other people's children; teachers, children's ministers, pre-school teachers. It is a hard thing to be around kids day in and day out when you are longing for one of your own. But even if it is hard, it doesn't mean it isn't immensely fruitful!

I helped a friend who had two stair-step babies. Every time we went shopping together people told me what a beautiful baby I had and I told them "I can't take the credit" as the knot in my stomach tightened. She needed me for that season and in my heart, I felt the Lord call me to serve Him, my friend and her little ones, even though it stung a bit.

> *Sometimes His plan includes those of us without kids of our own tending to His, regardless of the fact that they aren't "ours"*

As I picked up one of our students from church whose mom was so strung out on drugs she couldn't even get her own daughter to the doctor, I tried to push away the thought, "Why did she get a child, and not me?" I still don't know. But in the middle of it all, I know God has a plan - of that I am sure! And it is a plan of joy and a plan of significance.

Sometimes His plan includes those of us without kids of our own tending to His children. Are there any kids you know that need someone to fill in the gap for them? Is God calling you to fill in that gap?

Journaling your Journey ~

_____

_____

_____

_____

_____

_____

_____

_____

_____

_____

_____

_____

_____

_____

_____

_____

_____

_____

Day Six

Couple's Questions

Read through and respond to any or all of these questions this weekend. P.S.- My husband and I are praying for you!

1. After reading through the devotionals this week, which verses ministered the most to you?

2. How has this perspective changed your thinking about having and not having children?

3. How can you more actively seek God together in the midst of this circumstance?

4. How can you grow as individuals and as a couple for the purpose of being content with what God has given you now, while still preparing for a possible future family?

5. What Bible passage was the hardest for you to apply to your life and why?

6. Spend some time praying together about all the "nevers" that you feel have hung over your life.

Journaling your Journey ~

_____

_____

_____

_____

_____

_____

_____

_____

_____

_____

_____

_____

_____

_____

_____

_____

_____

_____

Day Seven
Scripture Prayers

Scripture prayers are not meant to be read mechanically to God. Rather, they are a springboard for you. God's Word carries great power. After all, He spoke the universe into existence. And when we pray using His Word to guide our requests we are aligning out hearts with His truth, His will, and His desires. So use these Scripture prayers as something of a "prayer launch pad."

Lord, Your word says that you are the One who enabled Eve and Ruth to conceive and give birth. I confess that life comes only from Your hand and that it is not within my ability to have children without Your intervention. Lord, thank You for being the Giver of life. Thank You for giving me life! And thank You for having a good plan for my spouse (insert name) and me in the midst of this season of waiting. (Genesis 4:1, Ruth 4:12-13)

Lord, Your word says that You took note of Sarah and that at the appointed time You gave Sarah and Abraham a baby (Genesis 21:1-2). Lord, please take note of me and my spouse (insert name) in Your appointed time. If you want us to have children, please help us to wait well, with faith. If you want us to be content and serve You as a couple without children, please take note of us and give us the grace to embrace this aspect of our lives with hearts that would honor You.

Father, Leah was a woman who sought the birth of children for a variety of her own purposes (Genesis 29:31-35).

Purify my heart so that I would have Your perspective on having children. Give me clean motives and desires that would honor You. Give me Your vision of what it means to raise children and remove "self" from my view of it all.

Lord God, Your word says that a barren woman can shout for joy because her children are more numerous than women who have a houseful of children (Isaiah 54:1). It is hard for me to imagine this. But Lord, please show me how this can be true for me. Please show me how You might want to use me in the lives of other children and teens; or, to have "spiritual children" as Paul referred to Timothy (1 Timothy 1:2). Lord, give me an open heart to You and Your purposes in this season that feels so empty. Make my life full with whatever You desire.

Journaling your Journey ~

_____
_____
_____
_____
_____
_____
_____
_____
_____
_____
_____
_____
_____
_____
_____
_____

Week Two

Theme: Finding my Identity and Direction in God's Word
Points to Ponder: Infertility has profound emotional impact
on the way we see ourselves and our life purpose. Rooting
our perspective in God's Word is our ultimate source of
hope and healing.

●————————————————●

Day One
Full in Him

*Or do you not know that your body is a temple of the Holy
Spirit who is in you, whom you have from God, and that
you are not your own? 1 Corinthians 6:19*

I (April) was talking with a friend I hadn't seen in quite
sometime about married life and the future prospect of
children. I told her my clock was ticking so loudly I felt
like the crocodile in Peter Pan - everywhere I went I was
sure you could hear the "tick, tick, tick;" my eyes
practically bulging in rhythm with the ticking! Much time
has past since that conversation and the desire for a family
has only grown. At times the emptiness of not having
children feels like the jaws of that same menacing
crocodile, opening wide and just about ready to swallow
me whole. I have literally gotten up from a dream about my
baby to check in on my little one only to get a few steps

away from the bed and remember, "Oh, yeah, I don't have any babies!"

It is moments like these that I have to remember what really defines me. It isn't what I have or don't have. It is the words of my Maker that define me. In the middle of the emptiness, I have to remember His Word says that I am full - not empty - full of His Spirit. Not having babies does not make any of us any less important or useful to God because His Word states that we are the chosen vessels for His Spirit to dwell. At the moments we are faced with the feeling of emptiness we can call upon the Holy Spirit within us to remind us of His truth and make us aware of our fullness in Him. May God's presence be very real to you this day.

> *It isn't what I have or don't have that defines me. It is the words of my Maker.*

Journaling your Journey ~

_____
_____
_____
_____
_____
_____
_____
_____
_____
_____
_____
_____
_____
_____
_____
_____
_____
_____
_____

Day Two
Made in His Image

Then God said, "Let us make man in our image, in our likeness"...So God created man in his own image, in the image of God he created him; male and female he created them. Genesis 1:26-27 (NIV)

I (April) was talking with a young woman who had some issues from child-hood; sexual-baggage-issues I could relate with all too well from my own life. She was telling me that if only she could get married she was sure having a husband would heal those ugly old wounds. I tried to dissuade her, but it was no use. The truth is that the deep and often complex relationship of marriage puts a bright spotlight on those kinds of wounds. And if you throw infertility in the mix, you might be in for quite an emotional roller coaster.

I was so sure I was past all that ugly old junk. I had worked through so much of it - and the process had been so exhausting that I was sure I was finished with it! Then when the reality of not having children began to sink in, it sank right into that old sore spot. I knew in my mind that the two circumstances were unrelated. But I didn't quite feel like that was true.

If your empty cradle is setting down hard on an old wound, you are worth every ounce of effort it takes to get healing and freedom from it!

As I child I had been told that the things that had happened to me were "my fault"- as if six year olds have fault in such matters. But those words started gnawing in the back of my mind again... "Was this my fault too?" If Satan can get you into a pit once, he'll try it again - and many times, his plan works! I was determined not to slip back.

Based on God's Word I can stare that old junk down and say, "You do not define me! I am made in the image of God - not the image of brokenness!" If your empty cradle is setting down hard on an old wound, you are worth every ounce of effort it takes to get healing and freedom from it! "It was for freedom that Christ set us free" (Galatians 5:1); don't miss one ounce of that freedom! When you look into the mirror do you see a person broken by sexual baggage or a person burdened by barrenness?

My prayer for you is that you might see a daughter (or son) who reflects the image of her (or his) Father! You are a child of royalty who is robed in salvation and wrapped in love! May His high calling for you define you rather than any brokenness or pain you've walked through.

Journaling your Journey ~

_____

_____

_____

_____

_____

_____

_____

_____

_____

_____

_____

_____

_____

_____

_____

_____

_____

_____

Day Three
Giving God the Last Word

It will no longer be said to you, "Forsaken," nor to your land will it any longer be said, "Desolate"; but you will be called, "My delight is in her," and your land, "Married"; for the LORD delights in you, and to Him your land will be married. Isaiah 62:4

Recently, two women were sharing their deep disappointment over their friends having more kids and their not being pregnant again - yes, *again*. Their struggle is certainly not to be discounted. But I (April) sat there thinking, "At least you have one!" I've read the Internet articles about infertility and know that without God's hand of intervention, the statistics say bearing children is probably out of the picture for us. It is easy for me to imagine life far off into the future and see myself in old-age, widowed with no family around me and get pretty good and down in the dumps. But, God's Word gives me two pieces of hope to hang onto when my thoughts turn gloomy. First, like we studied last week, all children are a gift from God's hand and some of us He just makes more keenly aware of that fact! So, I am praying and waiting for Him to provide instead of giving scientific research the last word on the matter. Secondly, over the desolate and barren places in our life God speaks these words over us:

It will no longer be said to you, "Forsaken," nor to your land will it any longer be said, "Desolate"; but you will be called, "My delight is in her," and your land, "Married"; for the LORD delights in you, and to Him your land will be married. Isaiah 62:4

There is hope! God will not leave us alone because He calls us into intimate relationship with Him. And over even the things in my life that say "Failure" "Broken" "Worthless" "Void" He will rename them "My Delight"! I am not on the other side of this, but I am hanging onto every ounce of encouragement and hope I can get from God! And over and over again His Word reveals that He is in the business of turning empty into full and victim to victor. Any one of us could get lost wandering the wasteland of our childless state. We could get depressed, bitter, angry. We could ruin our marriages or cut God off completely. But in the end, we would be the losers. So, I am choosing to hold onto God's character and His track record of goodness, sovereignty and His ability to turn any situation around. I am waiting to see what He does with this thing that feels so "Desolate" and what happens when He renames it "My Delight."

Journaling your Journey ~

_____

_____

_____

_____

_____

_____

_____

_____

_____

_____

_____

_____

_____

_____

_____

_____

_____

_____

_____

Day Four
I Will Give Thanks!

I will give thanks to you, for I am fearfully and wonderfully made; wonderful are your works, and my soul knows it very well. Psalm 139:14

All of us have days when we don't feel too thrilled with ourselves. And facing down infertility adds its own unique challenge to thanking God for the way He has made us. I (April) have a health problems which can, but do not necessarily, cause infertility. Not only might it be a factor in our empty cradle journey, but it also causes me a great deal of discomfort. Frankly, it's hard to give thanks to God for the way that part of me has been put together. Yet, His Word is clear that I am to be thankful, even for the things we don't fully understand.

With, or without children, we can stand on this verse and know that we are truly wonderfully made.
We bear the Master's signature and that is all that is required to be His masterpiece.

Since we are sure God only does things for our good (Romans 8:28), we are positive that our not having a baby is a good thing. Eric and I have discussed some of the reasons God might not be giving us a baby so that we can keep in perspective the truth that there is some good purpose behind this.

God alone knows what lies ahead of us. He alone knows what needs to grow or change in us so that we will be good parents. And in His good judgment I can give thanks for the way He has made me; and I can honestly say "wonderful are Your works." With, or without children, we can stand on this verse and know that we are complete and truly wonderfully made. We bear the Master's signature and that is all that is required to be His masterpiece. I hope you might know very well that His work is wonderful; and be able to thank Him with a sincere heart for the wonderful way He has chosen to fashion you and your life.

Journaling your Journey ~

_____

_____

_____

_____

_____

_____

_____

_____

_____

_____

_____

_____

_____

_____

_____

_____

_____

_____

_____

Day Five
The Key to Unlocking the Chains of Disappointment

"'For I know the plans that I have for you,' declares the LORD, "plans to prosper you and not to harm you, plans to give you a hope and a future." Jeremiah 29:11

Everyone quotes this verse. But most people don't comment on the context. The people of Israel heard these words from the Lord while they were in captivity. Their sin had opened them up for trouble and now they had been taken captive by the Babylonians (only to later have the Persians take over Babylon). It is in the middle of their captivity that the Lord speaks these hopeful words over His people. And in the very next breath God adjures His people to seek Him, promising to be found by them if only they would desire Him.

As we walk this road of not having children, our disappointments can threaten to take us captive. It can make it hard to seek the Lord if we allow our disappointment to get bigger than our God. Yet, in this verse there remains a key to unlock the chains of disappointment and disillusionment that may sometimes bind us. The key is expectation. If we are expecting God to work out His plans for a future and a hope then there isn't room in our hearts and minds for disillusionment and despair. God's good plan may or may not be to give us biological children. But I am confident that this part of my life is fully under God's control and that He had it planned from the beginning as a puzzle piece in the life of promise and hope He has called me (and you) to. Not having children is not a mistake. Not a failure. Not the absence of God working in our lives. It is somehow part of God's plan to give us a future and a hope. I can't say this concept always sits well with me. Worries, doubts and disappointment are a real temptation. But when I take those to God and seek Him in the midst of it all, as Jeremiah 29:12 suggests, I find the hopeful perspective that releases me from the captivity of my emotions. May you too find yourself wrapped in the hopefulness of His sovereignty as you seek His face and direction for your life.

> *Not having children is not a mistake. Not a failure. Not the absence of God working in our lives.*

Journaling your Journey ~

_____

_____

_____

_____

_____

_____

_____

_____

_____

_____

_____

_____

_____

_____

_____

_____

_____

_____

_____

Day Six
Couple's Questions

Read through and respond to any or all of these questions.

1. How has infertility affected the way you feel about yourself?

2. What verses from the devotionals this week gave you a more positive perspective based on God's Word?

3. Read the *Who I Am in Christ* list (next page). You might even want to print it out and keep it somewhere you can see it regularly.

4. How does God's goodness and sovereignty in the midst of your not having children help you see yourself and your life with hope and purpose?

5. Has your intimacy with your spouse been affected by the disappointment of not having children? How can you apply God's Word to this area of your marriage?

Journaling your Journey ~

_____

_____

_____

_____

_____

_____

_____

_____

_____

_____

_____

_____

_____

_____

_____

_____

_____

_____

_____

Who I am in Christ

I am the salt of the earth. Matthew 5:13
I am the light of the world. Matthew 5:14
I am a child of God. John 1:12
I am part of the true vine, a channel of Christ's life.
John 15:1,5
I am Christ's friend. John 15:15
I am chosen and appointed by Christ to bear His fruit.
John 15:16
I am a slave of righteousness. Romans 6:18
I am enslaved to God. Romans 6:22
I am a son of God; God is spiritually my Father.
Romans 8:14, 15; Galatians 3:26, 4:26
I am a joint heir with Christ, sharing His inheritance with Him.
Romans 8:17
I am a temple-a dwelling place - of God. His Spirit and His life
dwells in me.
1 Corinthians 12:27 Ephesians 5:30
I am a new creation. 2 Corinthians 5:17
I am reconciled to God and am a minister of reconciliation.
2 Corinthians 5:18, 19
I am a son of God and one in Christ. Galatians 3:26, 28
I am an heir of God since I am a son of God.
Galatians 4:6,7
I am a saint. Ephesians 1:1, 1 Corinthians 1:2; Philippians 1:1;
Colossians 1:2
I am God workmanship - His handiwork - born anew in Christ to
do His work. Ephesians 2:10
I am a fellow citizen with the rest of God's family.
Ephesians 2:19
I am a prisoner of Christ. Ephesians 3:1; 4:1
I am righteous and holy. Ephesians 4:24
I am a citizen of heaven, seated in heaven right now. Philippians
3:20, Ephesians 2:6
I am hidden with Christ in God. Colossians 3:3
I am an expression of the life of Christ because He is my life.
Colossians 3:4
I am chosen of God, holy and dearly loved.
Colossians 3:12; 1 Thessalonians 1:4

I am a son of light and not of sudden darkness.
1 Thessalonians 5:5
I am a holy partaker of a heavenly calling. Hebrews 3:1
I am a partaker of Christ; I share in His life.
Hebrews 3:14
I am one of God's living stones, being built up in Christ as a
spiritual house. 1 Peter 2:5
I am a chosen race, a royal priesthood, a holy nation, a people for
God's own possession.
1 Peter 2:9, 10
I am a stranger to this world in which I temporarily live.
1 Peter 2:11
I am an enemy of the devil 1 Peter 5:8
I am a child of God and I will resemble Christ when He returns.
1 John 5:18

Day Seven
Scripture Prayers

I will give thanks to you, for I am fearfully and wonderfully made; wonderful are your works, and my soul knows it very well (Psalm 139:14). Lord, please help me to see myself as You do. Please grant me the grace to be unswervingly convinced that I am defined by You and not by infertility, or any other "emptiness" that feels as though it hangs over my head. Please do a work in my life so that I would only have You seated on the throne of my heart in such a way that no one and no thing would ever have the right to define me. It is Your right alone, because you are my Creator.

Spend some time praying over how you see yourself and ask the Lord to write His truth on your heart so that you would be defined by the list above rather than anything else.

Journaling your Journey ~

_____

_____

_____

_____

_____

_____

_____

_____

_____

_____

_____

_____

_____

_____

_____

_____

_____

_____

_____

_____

Week Three

Theme: Where to put the Disappointment
Points to Ponder: Scripture records the struggle of many
people who wanted children. From them we can learn how
to maintain a healthy perspective on this painful topic.

Day One
Where to Put the Disappointment

*When the day came that Elkanah sacrificed, he would give
portions to Peninnah his wife and to all her sons and her
daughters; but to Hannah he would give a double portion,
for he loved Hannah, but the LORD had closed her womb.
Her rival, however, would provoke her bitterly to irritate
her, because the LORD had closed her womb. It happened
year after year, as often as she went up to the house of the
LORD, she would provoke her; so she wept and would not
eat. Then Elkanah her husband said to her, "Hannah, why
do you weep and why do you not eat and why is your heart
sad? Am I not better to you than ten sons?" Then Hannah
rose after eating and drinking in Shiloh. Now Eli the priest
was sitting on the seat by the doorpost of the temple of the
LORD. She, greatly distressed, prayed to the LORD and
wept bitterly. 1 Samuel 1:4-10*

Elkanah had two wives. One bore him children. The other
didn't. He was in love with Hannah, the barren wife. But

Peninnah, the other wife, provoked, taunted and incited Hannah to utter distress concerning her empty cradle.

In the middle of her distress, Hannah goes up to the temple during the yearly ceremony and pours out her disappointment before God. She was so totally wrapped up in her conversation with God that the onlooking priest was sure she must have been drunk and tried to throw her out. After she explained her situation, the priest prayed for her and some time later the Lord gave her a child.

The point of the story isn't *How to get Children in Two Easy Steps*. The point of the story is how Hannah handled her disappointment. How can we handle the mountain of disappointment that can pile up from watching friends and relatives fill their ranks with new babies? How can we endure it when others demean us for not having children (We could fill the pages of this devotional with the times people have said hurtful things... better that it is filled with Scripture, though, right?) How can we swallow watching someone who begrudges their children, or doesn't take good care of them, while we sit with empty arms?

Here's the answer: we follow Hannah's example; we take it to God. It doesn't matter if you took it to Him yesterday and feel like you are going to implode today. Take it again. Just because the subject matter is the same, doesn't mean that you don't need a fresh touch of truth or peace from Him again.

One day I (April) can find peace with not having children and the next I well up with tears as I talk to my girlfriend on the phone and hear her children playing in the background. Sometimes peace eludes me for a few days in a row. Sometimes I have a contentedness for weeks in a row. It doesn't matter where I am on the roller coaster, as long as I am faithful to take my emotions to the Lord. If I let those feelings fester inside me I will become emotionally crippled. I'll exclude myself from social gatherings where people bring their babies. I'll mess up my relationship with my husband. If I let it, the emotional struggle over not having children could invade every relationship I have, including totally hindering me in my relationship with Jesus.

If we don't faithfully process all the emotions that come along for the ride on this journey of infertility, our hearts, relationships and marriages could end up far more broken and empty than us just having an empty cradle

I know women who are so broken over not having children that they can't stand to be intimate with their husbands. Some women go on eating or shopping binges - and these can last decades considering how long the fight with infertility can last. Basically, by not faithfully processing with God the emotions that hitch-hike a ride on this journey with infertility, our lives can end up far more broken and empty than if we never had children at all

If you need a jumping off place to share your struggle with God; try these ideas:

1. *Journal.* Keep a prayer journal where you share your heart with God about all your feelings, baby related and not.

2. *Get out!* Go to the beach, mountains (my favorite), dessert, park or wherever you can find solitude and begin to talk it out with God mentally. When I go somewhere to meet with God I am not tempted to get distracted as much as when I am home; its just me and Him. Sometimes, if I can't get anywhere alone, I just jump in the car and pray to Him while I drive.

3. *Go to church.* Hannah went to the temple and the priest prayed for her. Maybe going down to the church and having your pastor or women's ministry leader pray for you will be a healthy release.

4. *Creatively express yourself.* If you paint, do ceramics, or play music use your talents to release that emotional tension. I have crocheted lots of baby blankets and prayed over the expectant family and baby as I crocheted. I would want someone to do the same for me when and if the time comes. Somehow that has been a healthy letting-it-go-to-God activity for me.

Journaling your Journey ~

_____

_____

_____

_____

_____

_____

_____

_____

_____

_____

_____

_____

_____

_____

_____

_____

_____

_____

_____

_____

Day Two
Go Ahead and Cry

David therefore inquired of God for the child; and David fasted and went and lay all night on the ground.

2 Samuel 12:16

It was David's darkest hour. He had made a series of extremely bad choices, and in the midst of them, got another man's wife pregnant. After taking this woman for his wife, the child was born. However, God was not pleased with David's actions or attitude and sent the prophet Nathan to inform him that consequences were coming. Part of the punishment was the infant's death. David threw himself on the ground, weeping, fasting and begging God for the life of his baby. After the baby died, David was comforted in his grief by knowing God was sovereign and that one day he would see his baby in heaven (2 Samuel 12:23).

While miscarriage and infant death are not automatically to be associated with punishment from God, we can learn something from David's response. David was not a perfect man, but Scripture records him as a man after God's own heart (1 Samuel 13:14). So what did he do during this tragedy? He prayed and he cried. He took his emotional pain to the throne room and leaned into the sovereignty of God.

I was just positive we had got the timing right and would find out we were pregnant soon! My cycle symptoms weren't normal and a couple ladies were sure I was pregnant. But, I wasn't. Based on my symptoms I speculated that there was a chance I had miscarried. Regardless of whether or not I had miscarried, my disappointment was no longer escapable. I had been working especially hard for a ministry project that had been tossed in my lap. I hadn't really wanted to do it, but tried to throw my all into serving the Lord through it. That day of disappointment I lifted my heart to heaven and said through my tears, "but Lord, I was serving You...but Lord..." I piled all my reasons for why He should have allowed me to be pregnant at the foot of His throne. It was at that time that I really allowed my heart to experience my grief over the emptiness.

> *Sometimes grief comes from something taken away, yet it can be just as real and even harder to articulate when it comes from something never given.*

Sometimes grief comes from something taken away, yet it can be just as real and even harder to articulate when it comes from something never given. I surrendered my broken heart to His sovereignty and found peace in His all-knowing and good plan for my life. I took a note from David's example and told myself, "It's OK, go ahead and cry" but then left it in His hands. I get a bit of comfort in the fact that David was a guy - and not just any guy, an amazing, tough warrior - and he still cried to the Lord. When you hit the wall of disappointment, there is no need to feel guilty, you can cry on God's shoulders - He's big enough to carry it all. Psalm 56:8 tells us that God collects each one of our tears in a bottle. Not a single tear you shed goes unnoticed by your Father in heaven. May you find peace and comfort as you lean into Him.

Journaling your Journey ~

_____

_____

_____

_____

_____

_____

_____

_____

_____

_____

_____

_____

_____

_____

_____

_____

_____

_____

_____

_____

Day Three
Don't Pin it on Your Spouse

Now when Rachel saw that she bore Jacob no children, she became jealous of her sister; and she said to Jacob, "Give me children, or else I die." Then Jacob's anger burned against Rachel, and he said, "Am I in the place of God, who has withheld from you the fruit of the womb?"
Genesis 30:1-2

Especially in our days of scientific technology, it can be very easy to pinpoint the culprit of infertility on one spouse or the other. He has low sperm count; she isn't ovulating correctly. And while God may be providing this information to help you, sometimes we use it in rather hurtful ways. I have listened to women blame their childless state on their husband's sperm count with such disdain and disrespect. It only takes one sperm to fertilize an egg, so if God wanted, your husband could have a sperm count of one and everything could work out. Don't blame your empty cradle on your spouse. He or she is not the giver of life! God is!

When Rachel said, "give me children, or else I die" she was actually making a much deeper statement than she realized. God gave her two children and at the birth of the second she did die.

That slaps some sober thinking into us (Eric and April).

The one time I grabbed my husband and said, "I need you to give me babies!" I could hear the echo of Rachel's words in my mind and recalled their fulfillment. My husband responded with his usual answer that we don't make babies, the Lord does. I quickly repented in my heart and thanked God for the place we were in; God is the One who knows what we can handle physically and emotionally. If He chooses not to give us children, we can be sure it is prompted by His goodness.

If you have struggled with blaming your spouse, ask God and your spouse to forgive you. Pray for God to change your thinking. And put all that disappointment in God's lap. He is the One who can take it.

Journaling your Journey ~

_____

_____

_____

_____

_____

_____

_____

_____

_____

_____

_____

_____

_____

_____

_____

_____

_____

_____

Day Four
Praying for a Baby

Isaac prayed to the LORD on behalf of his wife, because she was barren; and the LORD answered him and Rebekah his wife conceived. Genesis 25:21

There are many grey areas as to how we, as Christians, should handle infertility. Some of us are comfortable with a high level of scientific involvement, while some of us are not. However, in the midst of trying to discern how best to follow God, there are some clear cut black and white areas. Praying for a baby is one of these clear cut areas! In Scripture, multiple people prayed for babies and specifically multiple husbands prayed for God to give them children and God honored their prayer. If you haven't started praying together for a baby, get on your knees together!

> *Don't blame your empty cradle on your spouse. He or she is not the giver of life! God is!*

Isaac was forty when he married Rebekah and sixty when his twins came into the world. Scripture doesn't record how long he had been praying. God isn't a genie whose lamp you rub to get three wishes. Prayer is a gift to communicate freely with the Creator of the Universe, but it doesn't give us a free pass for whatever we want. Sometimes, the Lord wants us to keep praying for years and years before He finally gives us the answer we were looking for. Be encouraged, it took Isaac and Rebekah twenty years! Read Luke 18:1-8 for another encouraging story about hanging in there in your prayer life.

Journaling your Journey ~

_____

_____

_____

_____

_____

_____

_____

_____

_____

_____

_____

_____

_____

_____

_____

_____

_____

_____

Day Five
Don't Miss the Good

And we know that God causes all things to work together for good to those who love God, to those who are called according to His purpose. Romans 8:28

Trusting in God's goodness has been the central focus for nearly every devotional in this book! The first week of our study focused on the truth that God is the giver of children and that our focus should be shifted from all the things we need to do in order to get pregnant to simply focusing on the One who gives life in the first place. The second week of devotionals focused on how easy it can be to allow infertility to become the thing that defines us instead of looking to God and His Word to find our identity in Him. After two weeks of study that involved aligning our perspective with God's Word, this week we looked at some of the things we can do while we are in this waiting period. We can take our disappointment to God, we can give ourselves permission to cry, grieve and express our emotions to God. We saw one thing we shouldn't do - blame our spouse or expect him or her to fill God's shoes as the giver of babies. We also studied praying and how sometimes God wants us to hang in there for a long time with our prayers before He answers.

Today there is another thing we can do. We can choose to not miss the good! In every lump of coal that gets tossed our way in life there is a diamond waiting to be shined. So what is something good that can come out of this time of waiting? Well, my husband and I are doing our best to get his school debt all paid off (and I'll have you know that since the first writing of this devotional, with the Lord's help we did pay it off!). We also have taken this opportunity to do things we wouldn't do with kiddos. We went on a vacation with his grandparents that never would have accommodated babies. We enjoy the flexibility in our schedule to be spontaneous and go here or there just because we feel like it - something that would take planning and packing if we had babies. In intimacy we enjoy the privacy afforded us because it is just the two of us. I finished my masters degree, which had been put off so long that I wondered if I would ever get back to it. And I get to do things in ministry that would be very challenging with little ones needing my attention.

Childlessness does not equal the absence of God's work or presence in my life.

There are good things for us in this time of waiting. There are areas for us to grow as a couple and as individuals. There are dreams to pursue. Places to go. Wonderful adventures to be had. Don't miss the good in this season! Ask God to show you exactly how He wants you to spend this time. Appreciate each season you are in. And keep your eyes open for the treasures of goodness God has tucked into this time in your life. Look for the diamonds in the rough.

Journaling your Journey ~

Day Six
Couple's Questions

1. How might God be encouraging you and your spouse to give your disappointment to Him? Which of the ways suggested in day one of this week's devotional might you be able to employ in your walk with God through this season of waiting?

2. How might you have misplaced your disappointment over not having a baby (if you have) and what changes is God calling you to make?

3. How can you and and your spouse seek to pray more for God to provide a baby?

4. Brainstorm some of the ways you and your spouse can choose not to miss the good in areas such as: growth, goals, and fun as individuals and as a couple.

Journaling your Journey ~

_____

_____

_____

_____

_____

_____

_____

_____

_____

_____

_____

_____

_____

_____

_____

_____

_____

_____

_____

_____

Day Seven
Scripture Prayers

Lord, please forgive me for the times I have placed my spouse in the place You alone should occupy. Children do not come from my husband/wife, they come from You alone. Please guard our marriage from pointed fingers and the pain those kind of attitudes bring. Cleanse us from this tendency; grant us a fresh start. Thank You for the honest example of Rachel and Jacob (Genesis 30:1-2).

Father, grant us the grace to press into You in prayer over our empty cradle. Like the widowed woman in the parable (Luke 18) who was faithfully persistent, may we not be slack in coming to You. Lord, thank You for the way You are teaching us to seek You in the midst of this empty place. Father, thank You that in the middle of trying to figure all this out, I can know for certain that prayer is always the right response. Thank You for providing the gift of prayer. Thank You that You hear us always. Thank You that You do not tire of our prayers and that You are always listening.

Lord, thank You that You promise to work all things out for the good of those who love You and are called according to Your purpose (Romans 8:28). I can't always see how in the world this could ever be "good," but I am trusting in Your goodness. Thank You that You love me and that You have ordained even this situation to work according to Your purpose. There is nothing in my life that is outside Your touch. For that, I praise You! I trust You, my Lord.

Journaling your Journey ~

Week Four

Theme: Mining for the Gold During this Season of Waiting

Points to Ponder: If we are faithful to seek God during this time of waiting we will mine lasting gold for our lives so that this time will count for something!

●————————●

Day One
A Golden Opportunity

And he (Elisha) said to him, "Say now to her, 'Look, you have been concerned for us with all this care. What can I do for you? Do you want me to speak on your behalf to the king or to the commander of the army?'" She answered, "I dwell among my own people." So he said, "What then is to be done for her?" And Gehazi answered, "Actually, she has no son, and her husband is old." So he said, "Call her." When he had called her, she stood in the doorway. Then he said, "About this time next year you shall embrace a son." And she said, "No, my lord. Man of God, do not lie to your maidservant!" But the woman conceived, and bore a son when the appointed time had come, of which Elisha had told her. II Kings 4:13-17 (NKJ)

This week we will be studying ways that we can mine for the gold in this season of waiting. This woman from the passage above is an excellent example of getting the good out of every situation. She was married, well off financially, but childless. She decided to make one of the rooms of their house available for Elisha, whom she noticed traveled through their town often. He was a traveling prophet and she reached out to help him in his ministry.

Childlessness does not reflect emptiness. We all have something to give. During her time of waiting, she was faithful to serve with the resources she had available to her. In the midst of her service, Elisha's attention was turned toward her childless state. She never mentioned it to him. God used his servant, Gehazi, to tell Elisha about her need. And through her service and support to Elisha, she opened her life up for God's blessing. Shortly thereafter Elisha prayed for her to have a baby and her desire was finally granted.

This time of waiting was not designed for us to get really good at twiddling our thumbs. God has something for us to do! I wonder if the woman would have opened her home to Elisha if she had children in the house. There are people we have opened our home to that we would not have if we had kids to protect. Not only was she looking for opportunities to serve, but she was giving without strings attached. God sees our hearts. He knows the difference between the times we are serving Him freely with pure motives from the times we serve Him in an effort to get something back. How might God be challenging you to serve Him unconditionally with your time and resources during this season of waiting?

> *Childlessness does not reflect emptiness*

Opening your home to those you might not if you had kids around is one thing God might be calling you to do during this season of waiting. But there's another possibility we hope you will pray about as well - opening your heart to someone else's needy child. There are children all over the world who need water, clothes, food, to know about Jesus and to be educated. If you had a house full of children, it might not fit in your budget or your lifestyle, but right now, perhaps "adopting" a child in need can fit into your life. We support the ministry of Compassion International. They make it a priority to teach the Word of God as they minister to the basic needs of children in third world countries. Can you imagine if the over 7 million people in the U.S. alone who sought treatment for infertility adopted one of these Compassion children what a difference that could make in the world? Consider it. Pray about it. Be open to the Lord working through you, just as Elisha's faithful hostess served God by opening her heart and home to the simple needs of one man.

> *Can you imagine if the over 7 million people in the U.S. alone who sought treatment for infertility adopted one of these Compassion children what a difference that could make in the world?*

Journaling your Journey ~

Day Two
After the Wait...

It came about in due time, after Hannah had conceived, that she gave birth to a son; and she named him Samuel, saying "Because I have asked him of the LORD." 1 Samuel 1:20 (NAU)

Waiting is never fun and waiting for a baby can be very hard emotionally. Today we will look at two pieces of truth based on the above verse to brighten our perspective with hope.

1. *You are not alone in the struggle with infertility.* Not only are there many couples around us that share in our struggle, but Scripture tells the tales of other couples in the same boat. Hannah was one such woman; Sarah, Rebekah, Rachel, and Elizabeth also were some of the women of the Bible who waited a long time for God to give them children.

2. Sometimes, special children come after the wait! All these women listed gave birth to a very special child after their long wait. Samson's parents were also barren before God finally deemed that the time was ripe for their little son's arrival. Could it be that in some cases God uses a long season of waiting as a tool to prepare parents for His children that have uniquely special plans (as mentioned previously in this devotional)?

I don't know if any of us will eventually have babies. But I hope that we can find inspiration in the examples of the women in Scripture who waited well and whose heart's longing was answered.

May we one day join Hannah and say "because I asked this child of the Lord."

For a season I (April) kept a prayer journal in hopes of one day having children. I was an "oops" baby. As I grew up I felt like my whole life was a mistake, since I had been made keenly aware that my birth had been a mistake. If we ever do have children, biological or adopted, I want them to know they were wanted and prayed for before they ever came into existence. You might keep a prayer journal with prayers and blessings for your possible future children. I enjoyed keeping just such a journal for a season, but stopped when I felt the practice had fulfilled it's purpose. Or, if the prayer journal isn't for you, then perhaps you and your spouse could set aside some time to pray together.

Journaling your Journey ~

_____

_____

_____

_____

_____

_____

_____

_____

_____

_____

_____

_____

_____

_____

_____

_____

_____

_____

_____

_____

Day Three
Made Perfect in Weakness

"But He said to me, "My grace is sufficient for you, for my power is made perfect in weakness." Therefore I will boast all the more gladly about my weaknesses so that Christ's power may rest on me." 2 Corinthians 12:9

I (April) can't say I ever imagined I would write anything on infertility. In fact, I can confidently say I *never* thought I would. It isn't a fun topic. It is hard enough to think and process through your own emotions in light of Scripture without trying to share and package those thoughts in a way that might encourage others. Our journey along this road has been longer than some, but not as long as others. Someone else could do it, I reasoned. Someone better. But it seemed to be something God wanted me to do and eventually I sat down and began the process. I prayed. I cried. And then I prayed some more. Then I began getting a few responses here and there. Women were actually blessed by what God had impressed on my heart to write. I was unspeakably humbled as God reached through this place of emptiness and filled it with blessings for other people. It was a moment when I could truly say I will boast about my weakness because He is strong when I am weak. OK, maybe not boast, but definitely praise God through it.

As we focus on mining the gold out of this season, use the above verse as a template for Scripture prayer. Pray for God's grace to be sufficient in all your weakness - emotional, spiritual and physical. Pray for His power to be

80

made perfect in your weakness. Pray for His power to rest on you so that you might be glad about your weakness. And ask Him to use your circumstance to be a blessing to others. Some churches have support groups; maybe you could start a women's prayer circle for those who are childless. Or maybe God will want to use you to be a simple encouragement like these women were...

One woman asked me how life was going. I told her God had filled our lives full of good blessings and I was just scrambling to figure out how to juggle it all. She perked up and asked if we were pregnant. I wasn't super close to her and had not shared that we had been trying. My face quickly showed my disappointment and I quietly said, "No, no, we're not pregnant" as I lowered my head. She smiled knowingly at me and said, "Well, I'm not either!" A few words and a hug later, I had been greatly encouraged by her incredibly gracious answer. I am praying for her - I didn't know they had been trying either. Now we can both lift each other up to God!

Another woman also encouraged me in that same season. She shared that her and her hubby had been trying for years; opting to just wait on God and not tamper with all the scientific possibilities. Eventually her husband was offered two jobs at the same time. One was a very stable manager position with great pay and benefits. The other was a ministry position with not so great pay or benefits. They prayed about it and he took the ministry position. The very next month she got pregnant! If they already had kids or knew they were going to get pregnant her husband never would have taken the job. God had the timing all planned out! She was such a sweet encouragement to me.

Who knows who God might want *you* to encourage! May you see Him show up strong in your weakness today!

Journaling your Journey ~

_____

_____

_____

_____

_____

_____

_____

_____

_____

_____

_____

_____

_____

_____

_____

_____

_____

_____

_____

Day Four
His Work in Your Life

Jesus said to them, "My Father is always at his work to this very day, and I, too, am working." John 5:17 (NIV)

When I spend time with my friends who have children, I am tempted to see my life as far more empty than theirs. I go home to a quiet house, there are no toys littered across the floor (well, maybe a few cat and dog toys), no baby crying or toddler busily doing two-year-old things. And even though there are definitely moments I am grateful for that solace, there are times when the stillness of it all tempts me to wonder why God hasn't filled my life with the hustle and bustle of little ones.

I love John 5:17 because it reminds me that childlessness does not equal the absence of God's work or presence in my life. Earlier, we studied 1 Corinthians 6:19 which states, "Or do you not know that your body is a temple of the Holy Spirit who is in you, whom you have from God, and that you are not your own?" Our bodies are filled - not empty - because the very Spirit of the Most High has taken residence in the hearts of those who have asked for Jesus' forgiveness and believe that He is God who came to earth, lived a perfect life, suffered death in our place, was buried, and rose again. I am filled with God's Spirit and my life is full of the evidence of His work. Philippians 1:6 says, "He who began a good work in you will be faithful to complete it." Psalm 138:8 reminds us "The LORD will accomplish what concerns me." God is actively at work in our lives!

When I can see my empty cradle as something that has God's hand behind it, I can find peace in my heart.

What are the verses that bring peace to your heart? Which concepts that we have studied together helped you the most? Week one we saw how God is the giver of life and the One on whom we should focus; week two we discussed grounding our identity in what God says about us rather than our circumstances; week three we looked at some healthy things we could do during this time of waiting; and this last week we have looked into how we can mine the gold out of this circumstance. Look over those concepts and the verses with them and see which ones were most needful to you. Take 3 X 5 cards and write the verses that were most helpful and place them on your bathroom mirror, scheduler, computer or wherever you will see them often. May you always be reminded that God is lovingly working on your behalf!

Journaling your Journey ~

Day Five
Remembering

I will remember the deeds of the LORD; yes, I will remember your miracles of long ago. I will meditate on all your works and consider all your mighty deeds. Psalm 77:11-12 (NIV)

When I get to feeling blue about not having a baby, my hubby is the one who is so faithful to remind me to reel in my thoughts and set them in a better place. Whenever we start to get stuck in that rut of disappointment, remembering the right things will be the key to successfully moving forward.

Yesterday we talked about putting 3 X 5 cards with God's Word in places we will see them often. The two places we can set our thoughts when they begin to sink is in God's Word and in God's faithfulness.

Today, we want to challenge you to write about your journey of waiting. Record the lessons God has taught you and specifically the ways He has shown you His character, love and faithfulness. Then, if you like, we would love it if you would share your story with us.

We have so enjoyed our time "together." We have been praying for you and look forward to hearing about God's work in your life. If the Lord delivers a bundle of joy, we would love to rejoice with you!

Hope to hear from you soon!
With love and blessings,

Eric & April

Motl Ministries
Email us at: info@motlministries.org

Journaling your Journey ~

_____

_____

_____

_____

_____

_____

_____

_____

_____

_____

_____

_____

_____

_____

_____

_____

Day Six
Couple's Questions

1. What were the Scriptures covered in these devotionals or in your own personal study that have been most helpful to you during this time of waiting?

2. How has God revealed Himself to you through this circumstance?

3. How can you be a reminder of God's character, love and faithfulness to your spouse?

4. How can you and your spouse be a reminder of God's character, faithfulness and love to others around you who also might be struggling with a season of waiting?

Journaling your Journey ~

_____

_____

_____

_____

_____

_____

_____

_____

_____

_____

_____

_____

_____

_____

_____

_____

_____

Day Seven
Scripture Prayers

Father, thank You that You are always at work and that this place of waiting is not like a doctor's waiting room in my life, but rather a construction zone of activity! (John 5:17) Lord, please help me to see Your hand at work and also see how you want me to be actively participating in Your work in the lives of others around me as well. Help my spouse (insert name) and me to catch Your vision for this waiting season and to be busy about Your desire for our lives.

Lord, thank You for the way Your power is perfect in weakness (2 Corinthians 12:9). Thank You that You are showing up strong on our behalf when we admit out inabilities and need. Thank You for the way You plan to reach through this emptiness and do something good and beautiful with it. Grant us the grace to be open to the work of Your hand however You choose to display Your plan and power.

I will remember the deeds of the LORD; yes, I will remember your miracles of long ago. I will meditate on all your works and consider all your mighty deeds (Psalm 77:11-12). Father, thank You for the beautiful things You have done in my life (thank the Lord for your specific life experiences with Him) and for the precious things You have done in our life as a married couple (recount them together, thank God for each one). We thank You now for all that You have been, for all that You are teaching us about Your good and trustworthy character, and for all that You are going to do in our future. We love You, Lord. And we cast ourselves completely on Your goodness and mercy.

Journaling your Journey ~

_____

_____

_____

_____

_____

_____

_____

_____

_____

_____

_____

_____

_____

_____

_____

_____

_____

_____

_____

Journaling your Journey ~

_____

_____

_____

_____

_____

_____

_____

_____

_____

_____

_____

_____

_____

_____

_____

_____

_____

_____

Journaling your Journey ~

_____

_____

_____

_____

_____

_____

_____

_____

_____

_____

_____

_____

_____

_____

_____

_____

_____

_____

_____

Journaling your Journey ~

_____

_____

_____

_____

_____

_____

_____

_____

_____

_____

_____

_____

_____

_____

_____

_____

_____

_____

_____

_____

Journaling your Journey ~

_____

_____

_____

_____

_____

_____

_____

_____

_____

_____

_____

_____

_____

_____

_____

_____

_____

_____

_____

_____

Journaling your Journey ~

_____

_____

_____

_____

_____

_____

_____

_____

_____

_____

_____

_____

_____

_____

_____

_____

_____

_____

_____

_____

If you enjoyed this collection of devotionals you might enjoy other resources from
Motl Ministries as well!

Visit the website at www.MotlMinistries.org

Visit the website to schedule a teaching event at your church, check out the other marriage resources, sign-up for free weekly e-devos, or contact info@MotlMinistries.com for more information.

Looking forward to hearing from you!

Additional Resources

Walking with Jesus 101
One hundred and one days of devotionals growing your walk with God

Face to Face: Seeing God through the Eyes of those who met Him face to face (devotional)

My Reflection in His Eyes: Seeing Yourself as God Sees You
Seven-week women's Bible Study

Free to Flourish: Cultivating the Fruit of the Spirit
Ten-week women's Bible study

Keep in Touch!

Motl Ministries
www.MotlMinistries.org
Email us at: info@motlministries.org

14312988R00057

Made in the USA
Lexington, KY
06 November 2018